LAROUSSE

Picture Dictionary

English - French
français - anglais

Auteur / Author
Natacha Diaz

Illustrations / Art and characters
Peter Brophy

Direction d'édition / General editor
Valérie Katzaros

Aidée de / With help of
Agathe Morel

Conception graphique / Design
Sophie Compagne

Création et production des chansons / Songs written and produced
Steve Lemberg

Chansons interprétées par / Vocals
Ann Dawson, Monique Messine

Piano / Piano
Tommy James

Arrangements musicaux / Musical arrangements
Joe Baker

Enregistrement chez / Recorded at
Baker Boys Studios, New York

Remerciements à / Special thanks to
**Amanda Fernandez, Maria Elena Buria, Fabio Pinheiro,
Patricia Forde, Paul Ahr**

Fabrication / Production manager
Nicolas Perrier

Création et production / Creation and production management
Marc Menahem

Concept
SULA

© 2002 Larousse/VUEF

CD audio/audio CD
© Larousse/VUEF
Composition musicale/Musical composition
© 2002 Stephen H. Lemberg/Vashti Music, Inc. ASCAP All Rights Reserved

ISBN : 2-03-540175-5
Larousse / VUEF, Paris
Distributeur exclusif au Québec : Messageries ADP, 1751 Richardson, Montréal (Québec)

ISBN: 2-03-542095-4
Sales: Houghton Mifflin Company, Boston
Library of Congress CIP Data has been applied for.

Achevé d'imprimer par De Agostini
Dépôt légal : mai 2002

contents
sommaire

La découverte de l'anglais en s'amusant

Ce dictionnaire illustré français-anglais, anglais-français s'adresse aux enfants de 5 à 7 ans débutant l'anglais en seconde langue. Fondé sur l'utilisation des diverses facultés de l'enfant : voir, reconnaître, lire, parler, écouter, répéter, utiliser et écrire, il lui permet de découvrir de façon ludique et interactive les 250 premiers mots de l'anglais.

Chaque mot a été soigneusement choisi par des enseignants et est illustré en couleur. Les mots sont mis en situation dans 14 scènes quotidiennes familières à l'enfant. En outre, quatre planches d'activités pratiques lui permettent de vérifier l'acquisition et la compréhension du vocabulaire, en mettant l'accent sur l'utilisation des mots et la lecture.

À travers 6 chansons, le CD audio aide l'enfant à acquérir plus de vocabulaire de manière naturelle et interactive. Quatre de ces chansons se fondent sur l'association du geste au mot pour une meilleure assimilation du vocabulaire : le visage, le corps, les mouvements et le livre.

Un poster de huit pages propose des activités supplémentaires et des personnages à découper.

Le Picture dictionary, créé par des enseignants en petites classes, est un dictionnaire ludique, amusant, coloré et totalement adapté à l'enseignement de l'anglais pour les 5-7 ans.

Guide de prononciation anglais

Anglais	Français
th	z ou ç
a	**eille,** devant un mot
	a ou **eille** à l'intérieur d'un mot
e	i long, sauf à l'intérieur des mots
i	**aille,** sauf à l'intérieur des mots
o	euou
u	iou
y	i long ou **aille**
ch	tch
sh	ch

Having fun learning French

This dictionary is dedicated to English-speaking children who are just beginning to learn French as a new language. The teaching method was developed by experts, and uses a wide range of the young reader's capabilities: seeing, recognizing, reading, saying, hearing, using and writing.

Each word in the text was carefully chosen by early childhood teachers, and each is accompanied by a colorful picture. Words come « alive » in detailed scenes of everyday situations.

There are ten scenes, four collections of items and six songs. Learning is reinforced via repetition in eight hands – on activity pages – each of which emphasizes reading ability, comprehension, and language as experience.

With the help of music – the universal language – the sing-along CD helps youngsters acquire further vocabulary in a natural and interactive way. Four of the songs use Total Physical Response, an interactive method which encourages children to « perform » the words. These songs are Face, Body, Motion, and Book.

An eight-page poster offers more activities and provides free-standing characters to be cut out.

The « Picture dictionary » is a fun-filled, relevant, entertaining and colorful book created by experts in the fields of early childhood education and English as a second language.

French pronunciation guide

French	English
e	oe
i	long e
oi	wa
ou	double o
in / im	en
en / am	an
gn	nye

window
fenêtre

teddy bear
ours
en peluche

pillow
oreiller

door
porte

bed
lit

alarm
clock
réveil

mirror
miroir

lamp
lampe

6

my room
ma chambre

glass
verre

bottle
bouteille

knife
couteau

fork
fourchette

spoon
cuillère

plate
assiette

table
table

chair
chaise

8

bowl
bol

the kitchen
la cuisine

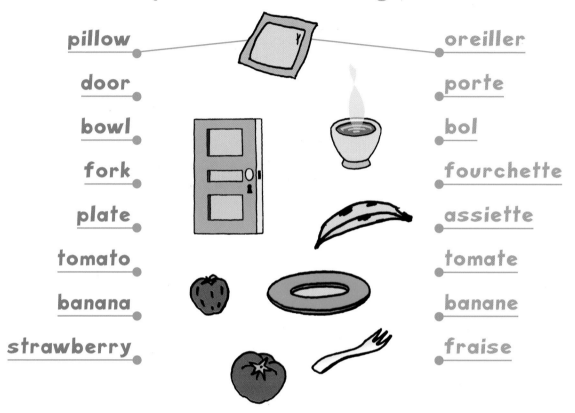

words and pictures

match each word to a picture
relie chaque mot à son image

pillow   oreiller

door   porte

bowl   bol

fork   fourchette

plate   assiette

tomato   tomate

banana   banane

strawberry   fraise

hidden words

find the following words
trouve les mots suivants

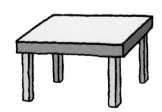

M	A	T	V	U	E	R
I	R	L	Y	G	B	O
R	T	A	B	L	E	N
R	I	S	N	A	D	N
O	E	T	L	S	O	I
R	R	M	G	S	T	N

E	T	T	A	B	L	E
I	B	V	S	R	I	P
J	A	E	H	C	T	N
V	U	R	U	T	G	A
M	I	R	O	I	R	T
O	N	E	L	D	B	F

les mots illustrés

match each word to a picture
relie chaque mot à son image

window

alarm clock

teddy bear

knife

spoon

apple

mushroom

orange

fenêtre

réveil

ours en peluche

couteau

cuillère

pomme

champignon

orange

les mots cachés

find the following words
trouve les mots suivants

C	H	A	I	R	C	P
R	U	D	I	V	A	S
I	B	N	Q	Y	R	F
S	I	P	O	E	R	G
D	T	L	E	M	O	N
M	N	R	A	K	T	U
A	P	P	L	E	S	X

A	B	T	D	I	F	P	B
F	H	C	I	T	R	O	N
C	H	A	I	S	E	M	O
I	T	P	N	L	G	M	F
C	A	R	O	T	T	E	S
U	X	M	C	P	V	S	I

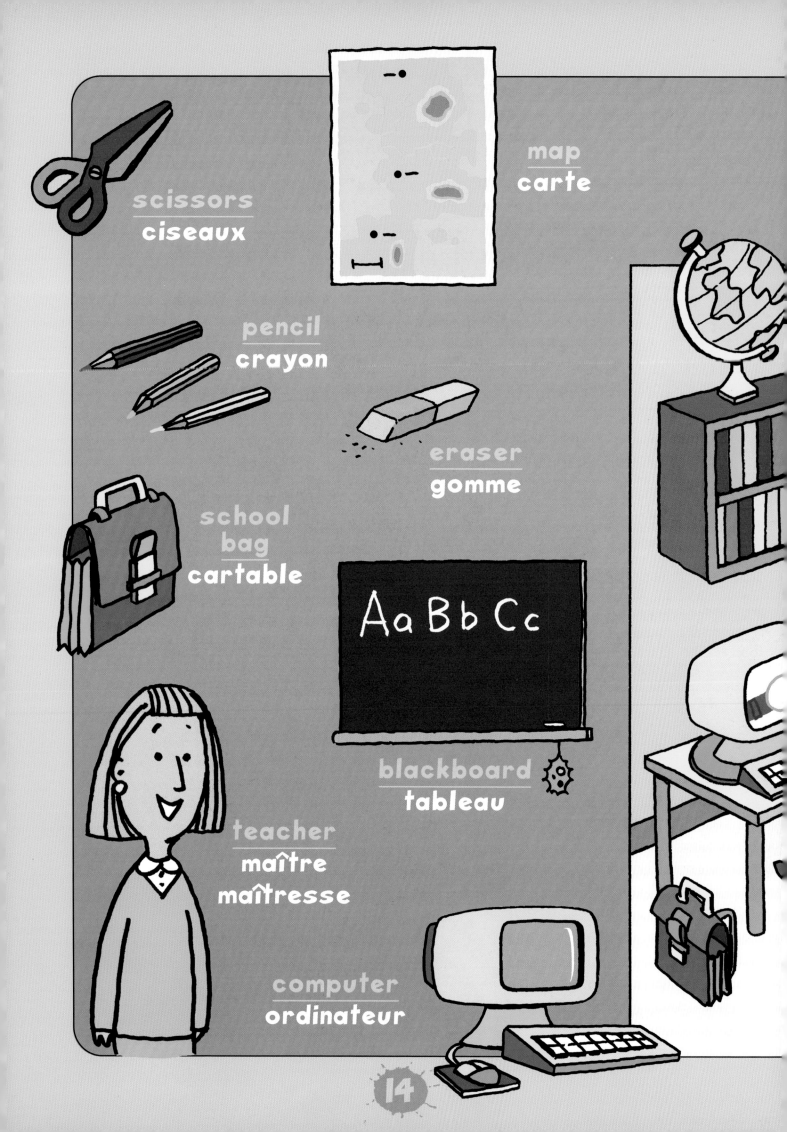

scissors
ciseaux

map
carte

pencil
crayon

eraser
gomme

school
bag
cartable

AaBbCc

blackboard
tableau

teacher
maître
maîtresse

computer
ordinateur

notebook
cahier

school
l'école

AaBbCc

doctor
médecin

astronaut
astronaute

painter
peintre

pilot
pilote

policeman
policier

dancer
danseuse

fireman
pompier

mechanic
mécanicien

les métiers

kite
cerf-
volant

puppet
marionnette

roller blades
rollers

train
train

mask
masque

robot
robot

balloon
ballon

books
livres

dice
dés

les jouets

scooter
trottinette

doll
poupée

crane
grue

puzzle
puzzle

tea set
dînette

baby carriage
landau

pencils
crayons

fill in the blanks

find the missing letters
trouve les lettres manquantes

teacher maître sse

- - l - e -
- l - d - -
 - - ll - r -

c - m - - t - - o - d - - - t - u -

s - o - t - r  t - - - ti - e - t -

m - s - c - a - m - - i - i - - e

e - as - r g - - m -

d - - t - r m - d - - i

p - - c - l -  c - - y - - -

draw a picture

join the dots
relie les pointillés

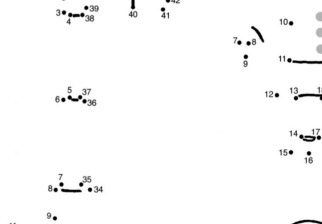

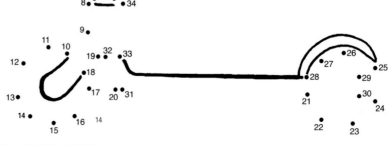

les mots à trous

find the missing letters
trouve les lettres manquantes

s-is--r-   c-s-a-x

--t--n--t   a--r---u-e

-o-ic-m--   p-li-i--

s-h--l b-g   -ar-a--e

k---   c-r-   --l--t

-l-ck--a-d   t----a-

--b-t   -o--t

d-c-   d--

à toi de dessiner

join the dots
relie les pointillés

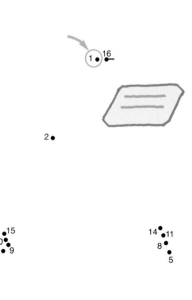

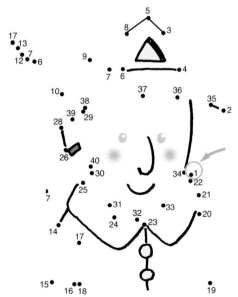

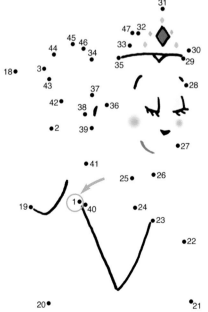

supermarket
supermarché

police station
poste de
police

shop
magasin

restaurant
restaurant

skyscraper
gratte-ciel

traffic light
feu rouge

street
rue

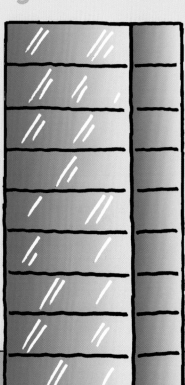

the town
la ville

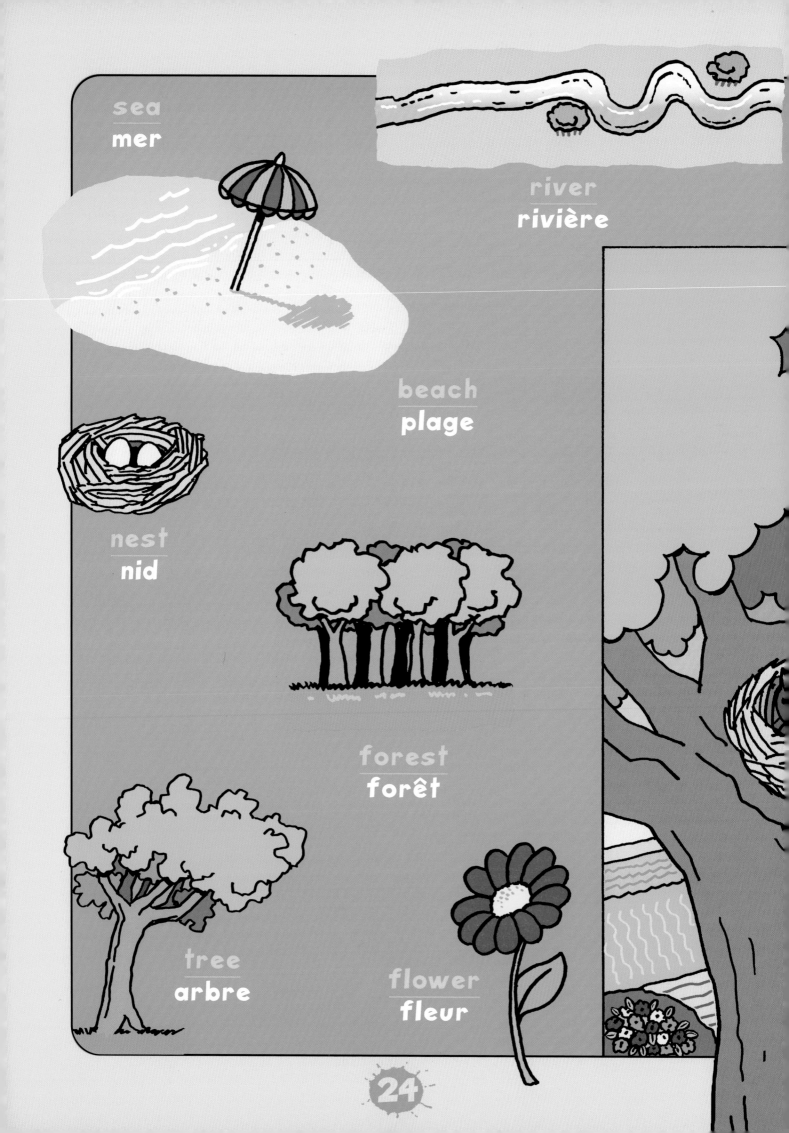

sea
mer

river
rivière

beach
plage

nest
nid

forest
forêt

tree
arbre

flower
fleur

24

mountain
montagne

squirrel
écureuil

giraffe
girafe

panda
panda

koala
koala

goldfish
poisson
rouge

elephant
éléphant

lion
lion

dog
chien

cat
chat

mouse
souris

animals  les animaux

crocodile
crocodile

dolphin
dauphin

penguin
pingouin

zebra
zèbre

tiger
tigre

gorilla
gorille

words and pictures

match each word to a picture
relie chaque mot à son image

supermarket — supermarché

traffic light — feu rouge

restaurant — restaurant

beach — plage

tree — arbre

mountain — montagne

koala — koala

cat — chat

hidden words

find the following words
trouve les mots suivants

M	V	T	S	O	K	J	R
S	Q	U	I	R	R	E	L
B	W	X	E	T	C	N	V
A	E	H	M	O	U	S	E
Z	S	T	Q	J	R	A	Q
N	H	P	I	Z	S	F	K
Q	O	F	O	R	E	S	T
D	P	Y	A	L	G	F	M

B	M	A	G	A	S	I	N	D
S	L	F	A	D	N	T	E	R
A	R	J	S	K	B	R	P	F
K	S	O	U	R	I	S	Q	O
T	E	G	X	A	T	H	M	R
D	F	E	L	N	L	B	Y	Ê
V	K	S	R	J	S	T	U	T
É	C	U	R	E	U	I	L	F

les mots illustrés

match each word to a picture

relie chaque mot à son image

Police station   Poste de police

skyscraper gratte-ciel

city hall mairie

nest nid

flower  fleur

dolphin dauphin

crocodile  crocodile

lion lion

les mots cachés

find the following words

trouve les mots suivants

L	R	I	V	E	R
D	L	A	P	M	N
O	S	Q	T	R	B
G	T	R	E	E	K
P	V	W	M	H	J
S	T	R	E	E	T

D	Q	T	S	K	I	R
S	N	R	U	E	J	I
R	T	S	Q	Z	A	V
C	H	I	E	N	B	I
B	F	C	O	Y	T	È
A	R	B	R	E	D	R
N	M	V	I	K	R	E

in love
amoureux

dreamy
rêveur

happy
heureux

shy
timide

sad
triste

afraid
apeuré

jealous
jaloux

angry
en colère

feelings
les sentiments

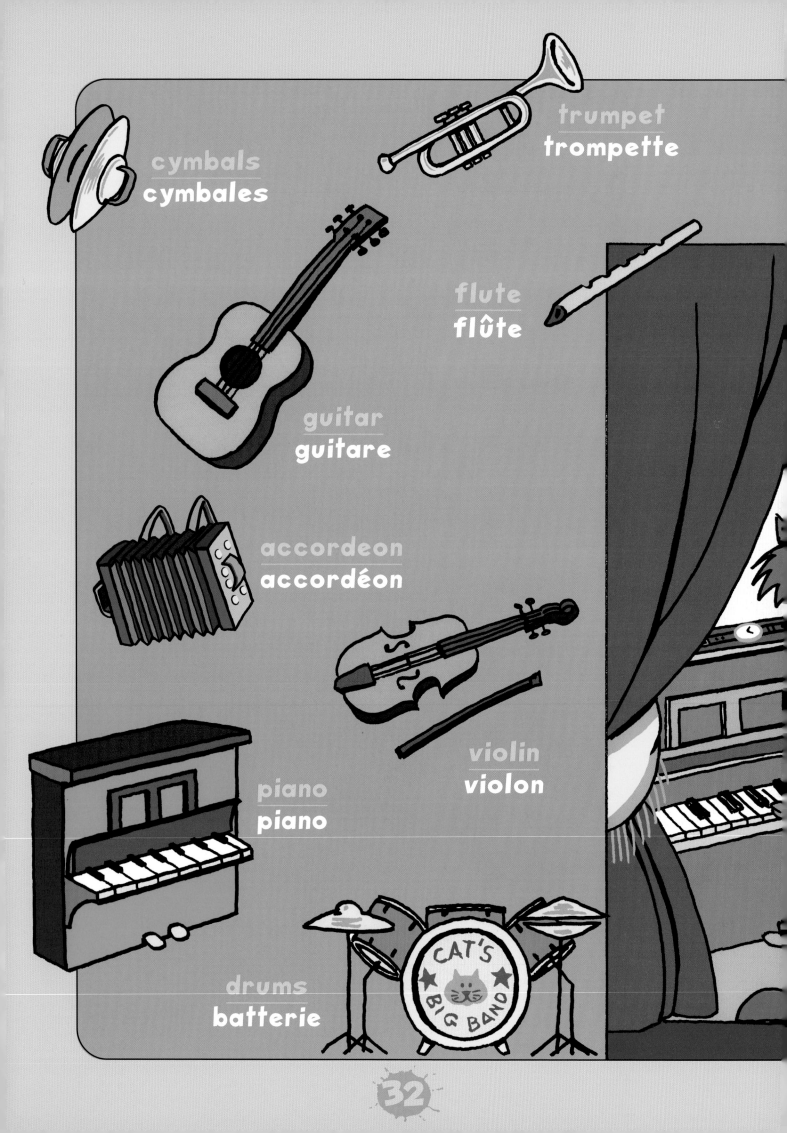

cymbals
cymbales

trumpet
trompette

flute
flûte

guitar
guitare

accordeon
accordéon

violin
violon

piano
piano

drums
batterie

CAT'S BIG BAND

musical instruments
les instruments

clothes

skirt
jupe

coat
manteau

jacket
veste

shorts
short

socks
chaussettes

underpants
culotte

shirt
chemise

cap
casquette

jeans
jean

shoes
chaussures

les vêtements

swimsuit
maillot
de bain

pyjamas
pyjama

gloves
gants

dress
robe

scarf
écharpe

fill in the blanks

find the missing letters
trouve les lettres manquantes

d-e--y -ê-e-r

-ng-y -n -o-èr-

-wi-s--t 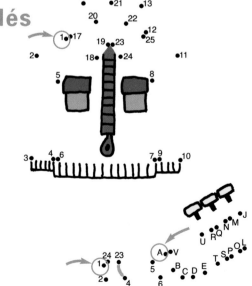 m--llo-
-e -a-n

u-d-rp-nt- -u--tt-

f-u-e  -lû--

-a-py h--re-x

a--a-d a-e-ré

s-o-s 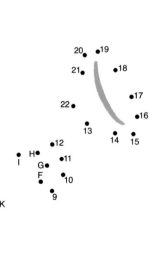 -ha-s--r-s

draw a picture

join the dots
relie les pointillés

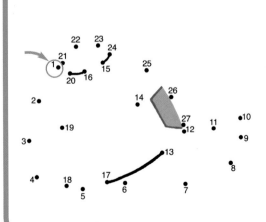

les mots à trous

find the missing letters
trouve les lettres manquantes

- -y   -im- -e

-y-b-ls   c-mb- -es

i- l- -e   -m-u-e-x

s-c-s   c-a- -s-tt-s

d- -m-   -at- -r-e

-lo- -s   g-nt-

v- -l-n   -i-l-n

s-d   t-i-t-

à toi de dessiner

join the dots
relie les pointillés

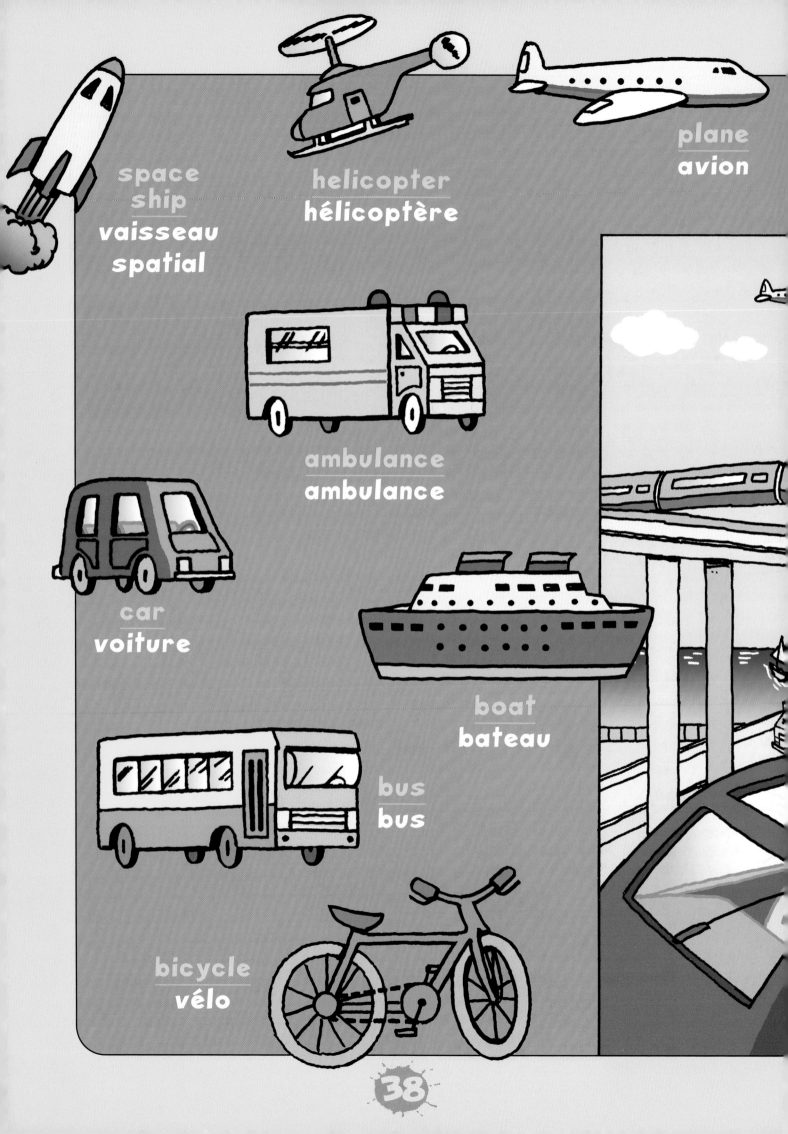

space
ship
**vaisseau
spatial**

helicopter
hélicoptère

plane
avion

ambulance
ambulance

car
voiture

boat
bateau

bus
bus

bicycle
vélo

transportation
les transports

sun
soleil

moon
lune

night
nuit

day
jour

rain
pluie

snow
neige

wind
vent

clouds
nuages

weather
le temps

the body
le corps

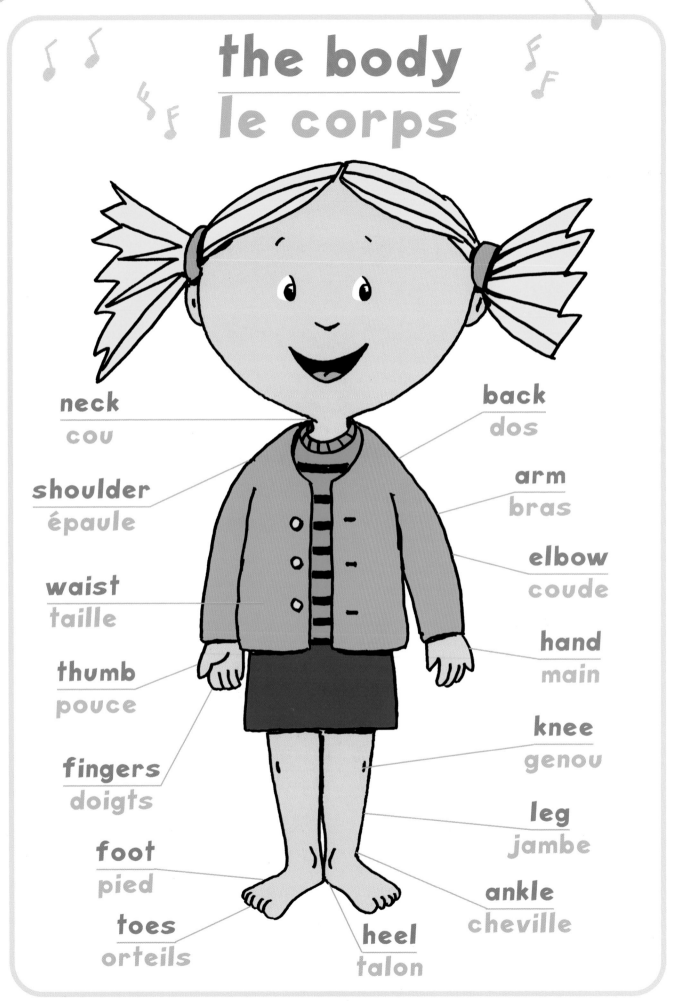

neck
cou

back
dos

shoulder
épaule

arm
bras

elbow
coude

waist
taille

thumb
pouce

hand
main

knee
genou

fingers
doigts

leg
jambe

foot
pied

ankle
cheville

toes
orteils

heel
talon

the face
le visage

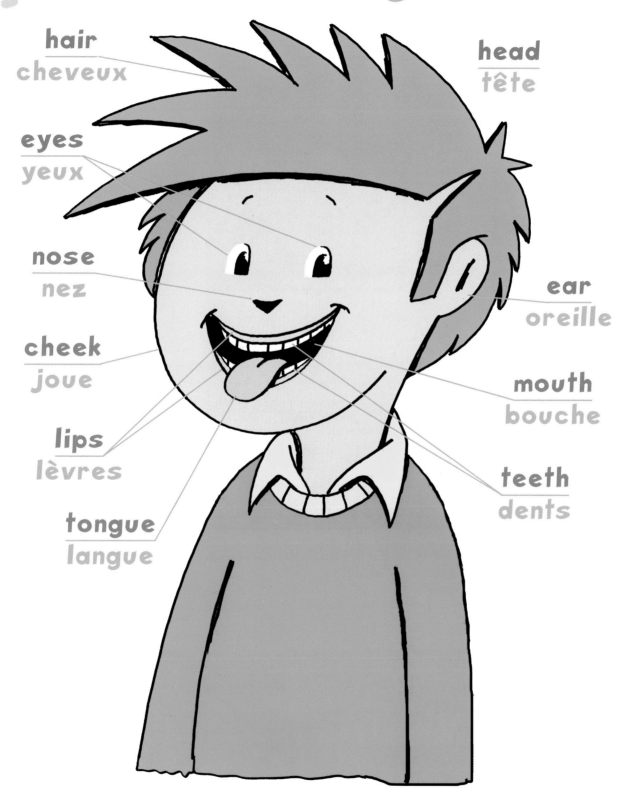

hair
cheveux

head
tête

eyes
yeux

nose
nez

ear
oreille

cheek
joue

mouth
bouche

lips
lèvres

teeth
dents

tongue
langue

greetings
les salutations

good morning
bonjour

hello
bonjour

how are you?
comment vas-tu?

fine thank you
bien merci

have a good day
bonne journée

good bye
au revoir

good bye
au revoir

good evening
bonsoir

good evening
bonsoir

good night
bonne nuit

happy birthday
joyeux anniversaire

motion
les mouvements

to clap
frapper dans ses mains

CLAP CLAP

to dance
danser

to point
montrer du doigt

HAHAHA

to laugh
rire

to turn
tourner

forward
avant

down
en bas

up
en haut

to jump
sauter

backward
arrière

left
gauche

right
droite

45

books
les livres

to open
ouvrir

to close
fermer

book
livre

to find
trouver

to read
lire

to look for
chercher

words
mots

picture
image

colors
les couleurs

orange
orange

yellow
jaune

blue
bleu

green
vert

red
rouge

grey
gris

black
noir

brown
brun

pink
rose

numbers
les chiffres

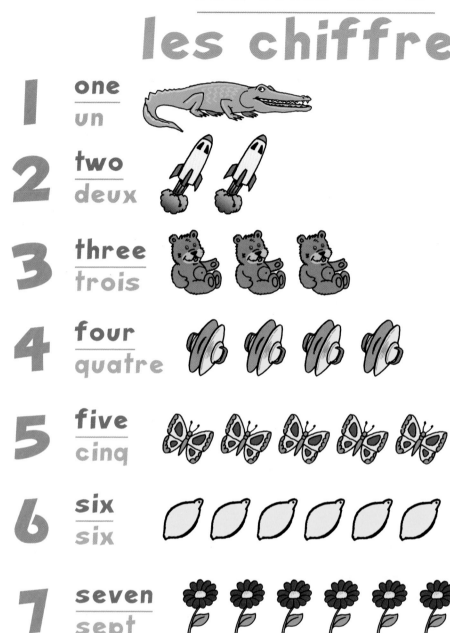

1 **one** / un

2 **two** / deux

3 **three** / trois

4 **four** / quatre

5 **five** / cinq

6 **six** / six

7 **seven** / sept

8 **eight** / huit

9 **nine** / neuf

10 **ten** / dix